Too Much Snow!

by Layne deMarin

Consultant:
Adria F. Klein, PhD
California State University, San Bernardino

CAPSTONE PRESS
a capstone imprint

Wonder Readers are published by Capstone Press,
1710 Roe Crest Drive, North Mankato, Minnesota 56003.
www.capstonepub.com

Books published by Capstone Press are manufactured with paper
containing at least 10 percent post-consumer waste.

Library of Congress Cataloging-in-Publication Data
deMarin, Layne.
   Too much snow! / Layne deMarin. — 1st ed.
      p. cm. — (Wonder readers)
   Includes index.
   ISBN 978-1-4296-7944-2 (paperback)
   ISBN 978-1-4296-8637-2 (library binding)
   1. Snow—Juvenile literature. I. Title.
   QC926.37.D46 2012
   551.57'84—dc23   2011022015

Summary: Simple text and photographs explain what
snow is and how dangerous blizzards can be.

Note to Parents and Teachers

The Wonder Readers: Science series supports national science standards. These
titles use text structures that support early readers, specifically with a close photo/
text match and glossary. Each book is perfectly leveled to support the reader at
the right reading level, and the topics are of high interest. Early readers will gain
success when they are presented with a book that is of interest to them and is
written at the appropriate level.

Printed in the United States of America in North Mankato, Minnesota.
102011   006405CGS12

Table of Contents

Snowflakes

Snowflakes are so small. They fall to the ground one by one. They don't make a sound.

Every snowflake has six sides.
But each snowflake has its own
special design. Each snowflake
is one of a kind.

Snowflakes are made of **ice crystals**. Ice crystals that don't hold much water make light, fluffy snowflakes. Ice crystals that hold more water make wet, heavy snowflakes.

All of these tiny frozen flakes can add up to a lot of snow. Then people have to use shovels to clear the sidewalks. The streets are cleaned off by snowplows.

Blizzards

A snowstorm happens when a lot of snow comes down and is blown around by strong wind. The biggest, most dangerous snowstorms are called **blizzards**.

Blizzards are dangerous because the air gets very, very cold. Blizzards also blow snow into huge **drifts**. The drifts block roads and doorways.

This car got stuck in the snow.
Sometimes drivers get **stranded**
in their cars during blizzards. They
have to wait there until someone
can rescue them.

Other drivers might get caught in a **whiteout**. This happens when a lot of snow is blowing in the air. It is hard to see. Drivers can't even see the road during a whiteout.

Storm Stories

In 1888, many people died in a big blizzard. It was one of the worst winter storms in history. People were not ready for the cold temperatures and all that snow.

Washington, D.C., had a huge blizzard in 2010. People remember how much work it was to dig out of all that snow.

Weather Warnings

In the past, scientists did not know how to predict the weather. That is why so many people died in blizzards and snowstorms. They didn't even know a storm was coming.

Today it is much different. Scientists and **meteorologists** have tools such as this radar dome that help them predict the weather. They can warn people about dangerous weather.

This scientist watches the weather every day. Scientists and meteorologists use computers, radar, and other tools to help them predict what weather is coming.

We cannot stop snow from falling.
But we can learn how to stay safe
when snowstorms are happening.
We can also learn how to have fun
when they are over!

Glossary

blizzard   a big storm with lots of snow and high winds

drift   snow blown by the wind into a huge pile

ice crystal   a tiny piece of ice that joins other pieces of ice to make a snowflake

meteorologist   a person who studies and predicts the weather

stranded   to be left in a strange or unsafe place without any way to escape

whiteout   a snowstorm with so much snow in the air that people can't see; everything looks white

Now Try This!

So many words rhyme with snow: grow, crow, slow, uh-oh ... How many more can you think of? Make a list, then use the words to write a poem about snow. For an extra challenge, pretend you're a weather forecaster. Write a rhyming forecast about a big winter storm that's coming. Hello, blowing snow!

Internet Sites

FactHound offers a safe, fun way to find Internet sites related to this book. All of the sites on FactHound have been researched by our staff.

Here's all you do:

Visit *www.facthound.com*

Type in this code: 9781429686372

Super-cool stuff! Check out projects, games and lots more at **www.capstonekids.com**

Index

Editorial Credits

Maryellen Gregoire, project director; Mary Lindeen, consulting editor; Gene Bentdahl, designer; Sarah Schuette, editor; Wanda Winch, media researcher; Eric Manske, production specialist

Photo Credits

AP Images: 14; Library of Congress: 12; Newscom: ZUMA Press/Kelly Owen, 16; Shutterstock: Anest, 5, Anne Kitzman, 8, Benedictus, 9, Dave Newman, 13, Dean Kerr, 15, Ioana Davies (Drutu), 4, Marijus Auruskevicius, 1, Oleksandr Kotendo, 6, Pavel Losevsky, 17, sematadesign, cover, stock_shot, 11, TranceDrumer, 10, Trudy Wilkerson, 7

Word Count: **369**   Guided Reading Level: K   Early Intervention Level: **19**